W9-BZB-039

History and Activities of the
Roman Empire

Alexandra Fix

Heinemann Library
Chicago, Illinois

Customer Service 888-454-2279
Visit our website at www.heinemannlibrary.com

Designed by Kimberly R. Miracle in collaboration with Cavedweller Studio
Originated by Chroma Graphics
Printed in China by WKT Company Limited

11 10 09 08 07
10 9 8 7 6 5 4 3 2 1

The Library of Congress has cataloged the first edition as follows:
Fix, Alexandra, 1950-
      History and activities of the Roman Empire / Alexandra Mary Fix.
          p. cm. -- (Hands-on ancient history)
      Includes bibliographical references and index.
      ISBN 1-4034-7924-0 (HC) -- ISBN 1-4034-7932-1 (PB)
      1. Rome--Social life and customs--Juvenile literature. I. Title. II. Series.

DG78.F54 2007
937--dc22   2005035172
13-digit ISBNs:
978-1-4034-7924-2 (hardcover)
978-1-4034-7932-7 (paperback)

Acknowledgments
The author and publishers are grateful to the following for permission to reproduce photographs: Ancient Art and Architecture Collection, p. **11**; Bridgeman Art Library, pp. **10** (Private Collection), **12** (Museo della Civilta Romana, Rome, Italy, Giraudon), **18** (Ephesus Museum, Turkey); Corbis, pp. **4** (Bob Krist), **7** (Richard T. Nowitz), **8** (Archivo Iconografico, S.A.), **9** (Vanni Archive), **13** (Nathan Benn), **14** (Araldo de Luca), **15** (Alinari Archives), **16** (Richard T. Nowitz), **22** (Gianni Dagli Orti); Getty Images, p. **26** (National Geographic).

Cover photographs of a Roman mosaic (foreground) reproduced with permission of Corbis/Araldo de Luca and the Colosseum (background) reproduced with permission of Getty Images/Photodisc.

The publishers would like to thank Greg Aldrete and Eric Utech for their assistance in the preparation of this book.

Every effort has been made to contact copyright holders of any material reproduced in this book. Any omissions will be rectified in subsequent printings if notice is given to the publisher.

Table of Contents

Some words are shown in bold, **like this**. You can find out what they mean by looking in the glossary.

Chapter 1: Rise and Fall of the Roman Empire

Rome was founded around 753 B.C.E. It was built on seven hills above the Tiber River in Italy. One thousand years later, it was the center of the largest, most powerful empire in the ancient world. The Romans' inventions and ideas still affect our lives today.

According to a Roman story, the god of war had twin sons. They were named Romulus and Remus, and they were raised by a female wolf. When they grew up, Romulus became leader of Rome. A man named Romulus really did become Rome's first king. Kings began to rule Rome in 753 B.C.E. Each king passed the rule on to his chosen follower.

By 509 B.C.E. many Romans were unhappy with the kings. They wanted to choose their ruler. So, they formed a **republic**. Now, instead of a king, there was a senate. Roman **citizens** voted for the senators. Each year two men were elected as consuls. They led the senate.

About dates

The phrases B.C. and B.C.E. show that something happened before Jesus was born. The phrases C.E. and A.D. show that something happened after Jesus was born. On this timeline you can see that Rome was founded 753 years before Jesus was born. The empire ended 476 years after Jesus's birth. With modern dates we do not usually use C.E. or A.D. Everyone assumes we are talking about today.

Timeline

753 B.C.E.
Rome is founded.

753–509 B.C.E.
Rome is a monarchy.

509–27 B.C.E.
Rome is a republic.

A portion of the Roman Colosseum still stands today. This huge stadium was once home to the famous gladiator fights.

59 b.c.e.
Julius Caesar is elected consul.

44 b.c.e.
Julius Caesar is killed.

27 b.c.e –14 c.e.
Augustus Caesar rules.

307 c.e.
Constantine becomes emperor.

27 b.c.e. – 476 c.e.
Rome is an empire.

476 c.e.
Roman Empire is defeated.

Constant fighting for power in the senate eventually weakened the **republic**. Julius Caesar, one of its last elected consuls, was killed by his enemies in 44 B.C.E. His murder drove the empire into disorder. In 27 B.C.E., Octavian became emperor. He was the adopted great-nephew of Julius Caesar. He was given a new name, Augustus, by the senate. He restored order and brought peace. From this point on, the emperor was the sole ruler of the entire Roman Empire. This was very different from the way the consuls had ruled.

Roman emperors wanted to rule the world. The Roman army was well organized and very successful. They kept enlarging the empire by defeating other countries. Each captured area became a Roman **province**. Walls and forts marked off these provinces and kept out enemies. Sometimes people actually felt safer after they were conquered by the Romans. Towns formed around the army camps.

Soldiers brought goods and ideas from the provinces back to Rome. Unusual foods, beautiful jewels, and strange animals were imported. Ideas about art, architecture, literature, and religion were also brought to Rome.

Romans worshipped many gods. When they conquered a country, they often added the gods of that country to their own. They offered prayers and gifts of sacrifice to the gods as they asked for favors.

All Romans paid taxes to support the army and to give tribute to the emperor.

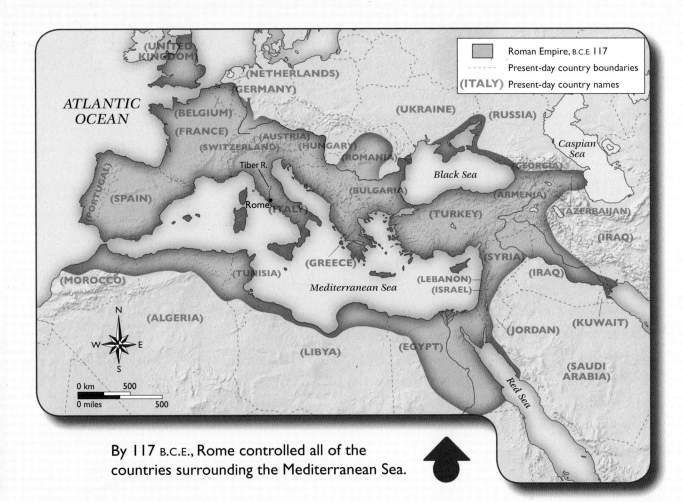

Map legend:

	Roman Empire, B.C.E. 117
- - -	Present-day country boundaries
(ITALY)	Present-day country names

By 117 B.C.E., Rome controlled all of the countries surrounding the Mediterranean Sea.

The end of the empire

The Roman empire lasted for about 500 years. Augustus was followed by more than 60 emperors. Among the most famous were Tiberius, Caligula, Claudius, Nero, Hadrian, Caracalla, Trajan, and Justinian. In 307 C.E., Constantine became emperor. He was the last strong emperor. After his death, his sons fought for power. This divided and weakened the empire again. Romans began to lose control in Britain, Gaul (modern-day France), North Africa, and Spain. The final downfall came in 476 C.E. A German named Odoacer removed the last Roman emperor and declared himself King of Italy.

Roman ideas we still use today

Under the Emperor Justinian, Romans recorded the principles behind their laws in a book called the Justinian Code. Those ideas still form the basis of the justice system in many countries around the world, including the United States and the United Kingdom.

Engineering ideas

The Romans were talented engineers. They built many roads between the city of Rome and its **provinces**. Roads were wide and straight so that army troops could march easily. Roman engineers designed buildings using new materials. They created concrete from a mixture of broken stones, lime, sand, volcanic ash, and water. The concrete was waterproof and especially good for bridges and **aqueducts**. Aqueducts were pipes that carried water downhill from mountain springs, miles away. Fresh water was delivered to public baths, town fountains, and some private homes. Romans built sewers with underground pumps and pipes, taking old water from fountains, baths, and toilets.

The arch was not new, but Romans expanded its use. Arches made it less costly to build long bridges and aqueducts.

This domed building could hold an imaginary ball as tall as a twelve-story building.

Romans built structures to celebrate their emperors, and temples to honor their gods. Using concrete and arches that crossed over each other, they created the dome.

The Pantheon is a temple with one of the largest concrete domes ever built. It still stands today.

One smaller engineering idea was perfecting the horizontal sundial. Sundials were used to tell time and are still used today as garden decorations.

Letters and language from Rome

The Roman alphabet, the same letters you are looking at now, is the most widely used alphabet today. More than a quarter of all English words have their roots in Latin, the language of ancient Rome. This includes everyday words, as well as medical, scientific, and legal words. Several languages are based on Latin, including French, Spanish, Italian, Portuguese, and Romanian. These are called the Romance languages. "Romance" comes from the word Roman.

Chapter 2: Roman Communities and Families

Cities were the center of Roman life. One million people lived in the city of Rome. Most people lived in apartment buildings up to six stories high. Ordinary families might have a single room. Middle-class families would have several rooms. Apartments were small, so people spent a lot of the day outdoors. People walked everywhere, and the narrow streets were crowded. Wheeled vehicles were banned during the day. Rome was dark, busy, noisy, and dangerous at night.

 Rome was a busy city where people lived, worked, relaxed, worshipped, and governed their community.

Social classes

Most Romans were plebians, common people who worked for others. Some were craftspersons, farmers, shepherds, or fishermen. Equites were **citizens** who owned the workshops, stores, and apartments.

Women and men got jobs in workshops, hotels, and shops. Children worked with their parents to bring in extra money. Patricians were wealthy, upper-class landowners. They often owned hundreds of slaves from conquered countries. Some slaves were well educated and worked as teachers, doctors, and clerks.

Roman citizens

In the United States and the United Kingdom everyone born in the country is a citizen. Many other people can become citizens. In ancient Rome only some men were citizens. Women could never become citizens. Children were not citizens, but boys became citizens at sixteen. Male slaves could be freed or buy their freedom and then become citizens. Sometimes, all of the men of a conquered community were given citizenship. At other times, only the rich were allowed to become citizens. Men in the **provinces** could also become citizens by joining the Roman army.

This stone relief shows a Roman butcher at work. He is cutting meat on a wooden chopping block, something still used in meat markets today.

Roman home life

The father was head of a Roman household. His wife, children, and slaves belonged to him. They had no rights of their own. Women cared for the home and family. Girls married as young as age twelve. Boys married a little older. Most families had two or three children. Male children were preferred.

Wealthier boys and girls were able to go to school beginning at age six. There were no public schools so parents hired a tutor. Students learned reading, writing, and arithmetic. Boys could attend school until age fourteen. Girls left school earlier to learn how to run a household from their mothers.

Keeping people happy

There were more poor Romans than rich Romans. Many people did not have jobs. Emperors worried that the poor Romans would become angry. They gave Roman **citizens** a portion of grain. They also gave them free entry to chariot races. Today, we sometimes say politicians confuse people with "bread and circuses." This means they take attention away from real problems. This phrase comes from the Roman practice described here.

Romans enjoyed their mealtimes. Family and friends would eat and talk together about news, sports, politics, art, and literature.

Food and clothing

Romans ate a light breakfast of bread and cheese. At lunch they might add meat and fruit. The main meal was eaten in the late afternoon. This was often a simple meat or vegetable stew. It was cooked in the apartment or purchased from a food stand.

Most Roman men wore a sleeveless knee-length tunic. For important occasions they would wear a toga. Women wore simple, full-length white tunics. They might drape a colored shawl over their dress. Sandals were the most common footwear.

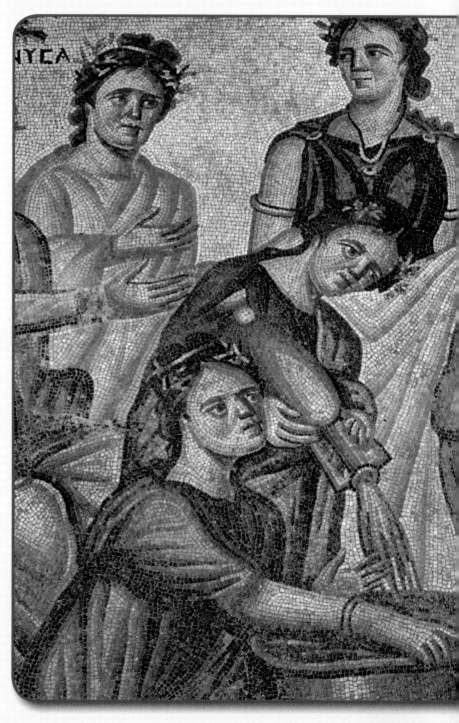

Mosaics in homes and public buildings often showed scenes from the everyday life of wealthy Romans.

Chapter 3: Roman Fun

Roman children played with toys we would recognize today. They had kites, hoops, tops, blocks, and dolls. A favorite board game was draughts, which is similar to checkers. Dice games and coin tosses were popular. One game, called knucklebones, used small animal bones as dice. Jacks as played by throwing stones up and catching them on the back of the hand. Children also played ball games.

For entertainment, many Romans enjoyed theater, storytellers, musicians, puppeteers, acrobats, and performing animals. Romans liked watching and joining in sports such as wrestling and track and field events.

In the center of Rome's hills was the Forum. It was a large, public gathering space. In and around the Forum were government buildings, libraries, gardens, and temples for the community. The public baths were very popular places to meet friends, relax, exercise, or even hold business meetings.

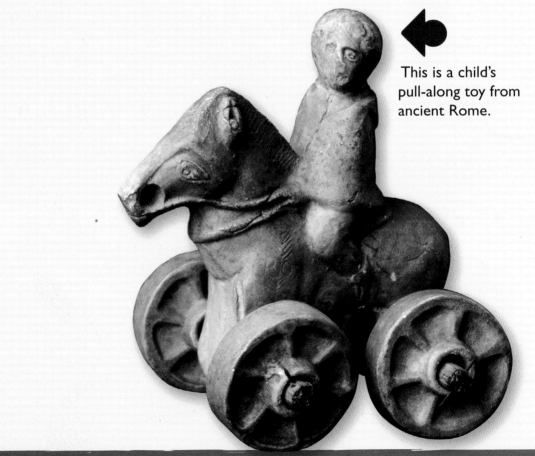

This is a child's pull-along toy from ancient Rome.

More than 100 festivals were celebrated each year. They were in honor of Roman gods and goddesses. The emperor hosted days of chariot races. The Circus Maximus was a favorite racetrack. It was a stadium that held 250,000 spectators. The crowds loved these dangerous, high-speed races, but fights often broke out among the fans.

Gladiator contests were also popular. They were held at the Colosseum. Trained fighters fought against each other. Elevators might suddenly bring wild beasts up from cages below to face a single gladiator. Most gladiators were slaves or criminals who were forced to be gladiators. Some free men signed on, hoping to win prize money. There were even a few female gladiators.

Roman fans cheered for their favorite gladiators, just as we root for athletes today.

By doing the hands-on activities and crafts in this chapter, you'll get a feel for what life was like for people who lived and worked in the Roman Empire.

Recipe: Libum (sacrificial cake)

Libum is a special Roman cake soaked with honey. It was sometimes offered as a sacrifice to the gods who protected Roman homes. A copy of this recipe exists from ancient Roman times. It is found in a collection of simple recipes for farmers written by Cato. He was one of the Roman consuls, or leaders, when Rome was a **republic**.

Ingredients and Supplies

- Wooden spoon
- 2 mixing bowls
- Cookie sheet
- 1 cup (8 ounces) plain, all-purpose flour
- 1 cup (8 ounces) ricotta cheese
- 1 egg, beaten
- 1/2 cup (4 ounces) honey

Bricks form an arch over the opening of this ancient Roman oven, found in Pompeii, Italy.

Roman Libum (cheese cake soaked with honey)
(serves four)

1 Preheat oven to 425°F (218°C)

2 Measure flour into a bowl.

3 In another bowl, stir the cheese with a wooden spoon until it is soft.

4 Add the egg to the cheese and beat the mixture with a wooden spoon.

5 Pour the egg and cheese mixture into the flour.

6 Stir the mixture into a soft dough and divide into four pieces.

7 Form each piece into a cake and place it on a greased cookie sheet.

8 Cover the cakes* and bake for 35–40 minutes or until golden brown.

9 Remove the cakes from the oven and cool slightly.

10 Warm the honey and pour it into a serving dish.

11 Place the warm cakes into the honey, so that they absorb the honey.

12 Allow the cakes to soak in the honey for 30 minutes before serving.

*The Romans often covered their food while it was cooking with a domed clay cover called a *testo*. You can use an overturned clay pot, a metal bowl, a casserole dish, or a foil tent as a cover.

Roman Libum

Wash your hands well if you plan to eat your libum Roman-style. The Romans did not use silverware. Instead they ate with their hands.

Craft: Make a Horizontal Sundial

Sundials tell time by measuring shadows cast by the sun on markers each hour of the day. Even though the Egyptians used it first, the Romans improved the horizontal sundial. Romans also invented a portable sundial for travelers. They were also first to use sundials in their gardens.

Warning!
Read all the directions before beginning the project.

The Latin words *carpe diem* were often carved on Roman sundials. *Carpe diem* means "seize the day." This reminds us to make good use of each day.

Supplies:

- Polymer clay (like Fimo or Sculpty)
- Strong glue
- 1 chopstick
- Ceramic plant saucer
- Protractor
- Pencil
- Masking tape or chalk
- Acrylic or other waterproof paint and brush

❶ Consult an atlas to determine the latitude where you live.

❷ Roll a small ball of clay and stick it on the end of a chopstick. Turn the ceramic saucer upside down and press the clay onto the center. Use the protractor to angle the chopstick pointer, called a *gnomon*, to the same degree latitude as where you live. (See Picture A)

❸ Remove the clay and the *gnomon* from the saucer, but do not change the shape of the clay. Have an adult bake the clay according to its directions. Then glue the *gnomon* back in place and glue the clay to the saucer.

❹ Take the sundial outside and place it on a level spot. Turn the sundial so the *gnomon* points north. At noon, use a pencil to mark where the *gnomon* makes a shadow on the perimeter of the saucer.

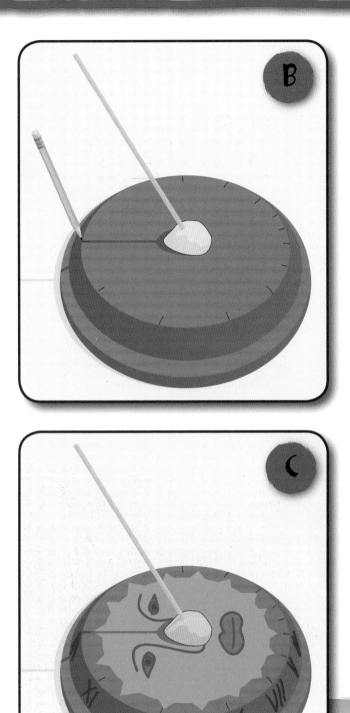

5 Do not move your sundial! Every hour, make another mark where the *gnomon's* shadow falls on the edge of the saucer. (See Picture B)

6 Mark your sundial's original position with masking tape or chalk so that you can put it back right later. Bring your sundial inside. Use paints to show where you marked the hours and to decorate your sundial. (See Picture C)

7 Place your sundial back in its original position. It will remain accurate until the hours change for daylight savings or standard time. When the time comes to change the hours, carefully rotate the entire saucer at 12 noon, just enough to make the *gnomon* shadow fall on noon once again.

How would your life be different if you did not have clocks and watches? Wouldn't it be fun to try going for one whole day without using a clock? How would you know when to eat or sleep or play?

Sundial

Sundials were one of the first types of clocks. You can keep track of time with a sundial by measuring where the shadows fall.

Where to put your sundial

There are two tricks to placing a sundial. One is to mount it outside at the correct angle to the earth. This angle (between 24 and 49 degrees for most of the United States) is the same as the latitude where you live. You can discover your latitude by consulting an atlas. The other trick is to align the sundial with True North, which can vary from the magnetic north that a compass will show. True North is a navigational term referring to the direction of the North Pole in relation to where you are. To determine True North, find a level spot where you will place your sundial when you are finished making it. Place a pole or stick upright in the ground on this spot. On a sunny day, mark the end of the pole's shadow every 15 minutes throughout the middle part of the day. Notice where the shadow is the shortest, and stretch a string or rope from the bottom of the pole to this mark. This line points directly to the north, from the pole to your mark. Note this orientation so you will know where to place your sundial later.

This ancient Roman mosaic shows a man leading a strong horse into an amphitheater for a chariot race.

Warning!
Make sure to read all the directions before beginning the project.

Craft: Create a Mosaic

Wealthy Romans decorated their floors and walls with mosaics. Mosaics were created with small pieces of tile, stone, or glass placed into plaster. When viewed from a distance, the colored pieces made a picture. Some mosaics were very strong and lasted for hundreds of years. One reason that we know so much about ancient Roman life is that the mosaics from Pompeii survived under the volcanic ash that buried the city. When archeologists discovered the mosaics, they saw pictures of what life was like almost 2,000 years ago.

Supplies:
- Drawing paper and pencil
- Assorted colors of paper or felt, cut into small pieces (if you prefer, you can buy actual mosaic pieces at craft stores)
- Scissors
- Glue
- Ruler
- Cardboard (optional)

1. Line the edge of your ruler up with one edge of the paper so that you can draw along the other edge of the ruler. Do this on all four sides of your paper so you have a frame around the edge. (See Picture A)

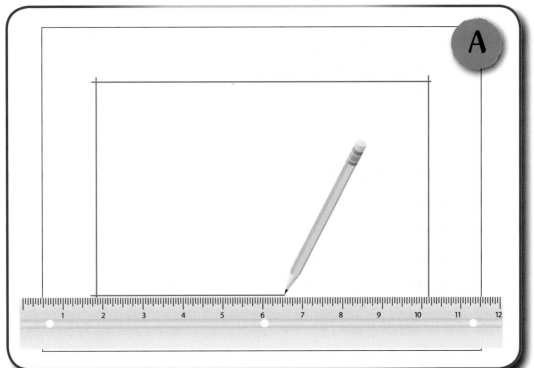

2. Decorate the frame by drawing a pattern. (See Picture B)

3 Draw a scene of people, animals, nature, architecture, or your own idea inside the frame.

4 Optional step: glue your drawing to a piece of cardboard.

5 Carefully glue the pieces of colored paper or felt to your drawing so that you fill in spaces one at a time. Use colors that make sense so that other people will understand your picture. Do not forget to fill the frame pattern with colors as well! (See Picture C)

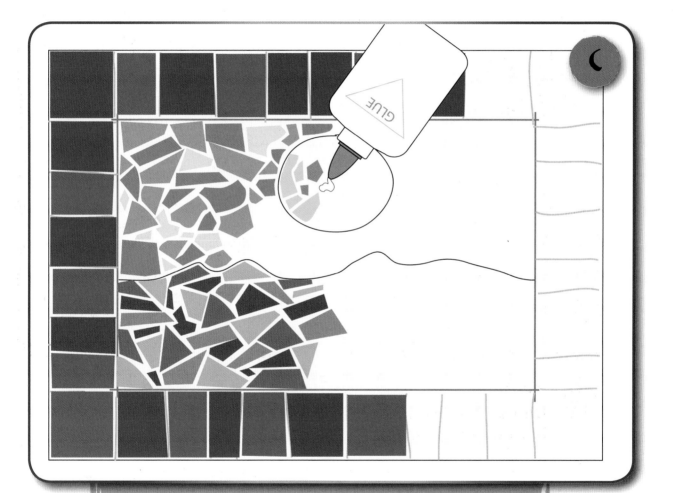

Hints:
You can fill curved spaces by angling the pieces as you place them side-by-side.

You can make your mosaic look even more authentic if you leave a small space between each piece of paper or felt.

 Mosaic

Use your finished mosaic to decorate a wall in your home. Roman mosaics often filled an entire wall.

What scene did you draw? What scene would a Roman child draw? What might be the differences between the two drawings? What might surprise you about the Roman child's drawing?

Craft & Activity: Roman Dice Games

Roman children enjoyed playing games with dice. It was fun to see who would be lucky enough to roll the highest score.

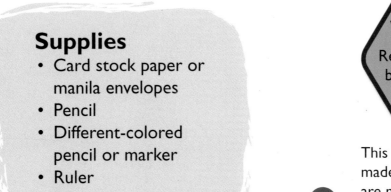

Supplies
- Card stock paper or manila envelopes
- Pencil
- Different-colored pencil or marker
- Ruler
- Scissors
- Tape

Warning!
Read all directions before beginning the project.

This Roman gameboard is made of wood. The dice are made from bones and the game pieces are made of amber stone.

What are some of your favorite board games? How does playing a board game differ from playing computer and video games?

1 Copy the pattern of a hexamine on to the stock paper. If you want, make a photocopy of the pattern below, cut it out, and tape it to the stock paper. You may wish to enlarge the photocopy before cutting it out. (See Picture A)

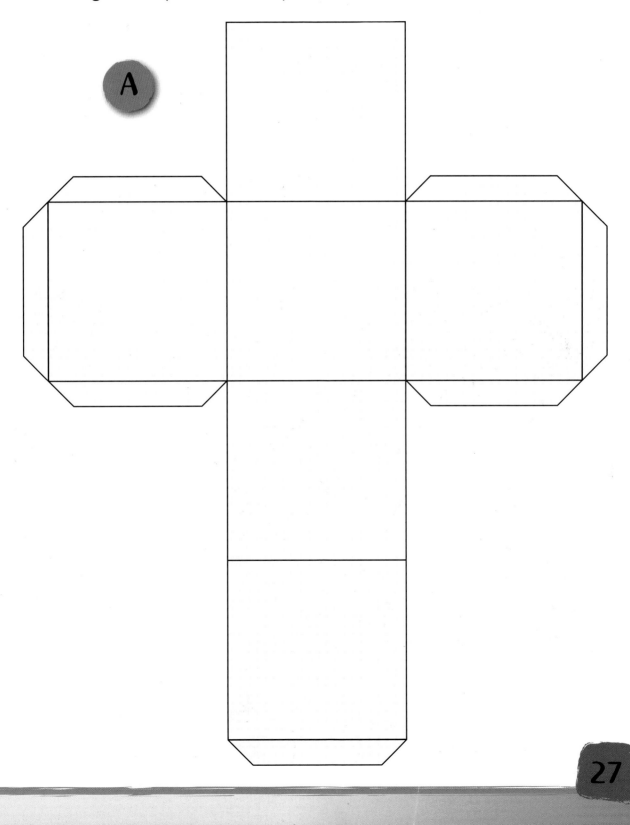

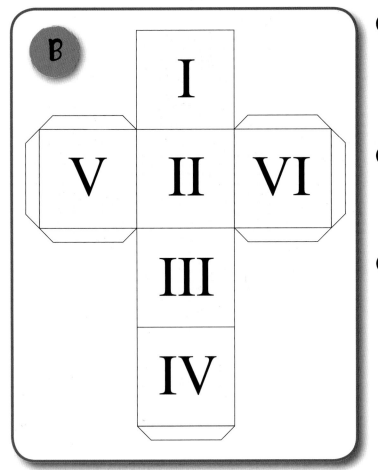

2 Write the Roman numerals 1–6 (I, II, III, IV, V, VI) on the squares of the pattern. (See Picture B)

3 The rectangle shapes at the ends of the pattern are your tabs for holding the die together.

4 Carefully cut the hexamine out of the stock paper. Fold along the lines of the squares so that you create a six-sided die. Tape the tabs down to hold the die together. (See Picture C)

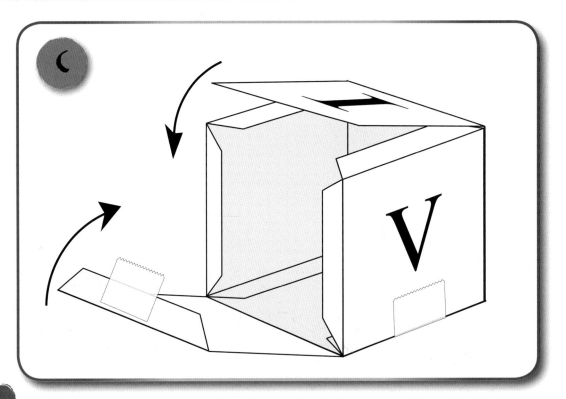

How to play "Pig"

This game is similar to games played in ancient Rome.

Goal: The first player to get a total of 100 points wins.
Number of players: 2 or more
Supplies: Paper for keeping score, six-sided die

- On his or her turn, a player continues to roll the die and add up the points of each roll.
- A player's turn continues until either:
    - a 1 is rolled, or
    - the player chooses to hold and stop rolling.
- If a 1 is rolled, the player's turn ends and no points are earned.
- If the player chooses to hold (stop rolling), all of the points rolled during that turn are added to his or her score. Play continues until one player reaches 100.

How do you decide when to keep rolling and when to hold?

Dice

When you roll a pair of ones with dice, people call this "snake eyes." Does a pair of Roman numeral ones look like snake eyes to you?

Glossary

aqueduct structure for carrying water

citizen person who is a member of a country and has certain rights and duties to that country

province parts of a country that are away from the main area

republic form of government in ancient Rome with senators elected by the citizens

More Books To Read

Lassieur, Allison. *The Ancient Romans (People of the Ancient World* series). New York: Franklin Watts. 2004.

Markel, Rita J. *Your Travel Guide to Ancient Rome.* Minneapolis: Lerner. 2004.

Tames, Richard. *Ancient Roman Children (People in the Past* series). Chicago: Heinemann Library. 2003.

The instructions for these projects are designed to allow students to work as independently as possible. However, it is always a good idea to make a prototype before assigning any project so that students can see how their own work will look when completed. Prior to introducing these projects, teachers should collect and prepare the materials and be ready for any modifications that may be necessary. Participating in the project-making process will help teachers understand the directions and be ready to assist students with difficult steps. Teachers might also choose to adapt or modify the projects to better suit the needs of an individual student or class. No one knows what levels of achievement students will reach better than their teacher.

While it is preferable for students to work as independently as possible, there is some flexibility in regards to project materials and tools. They can vary according to what is available. For instance, while standard white glue may be most familiar to students, there might be times when a teacher will choose to speed up a project by using a hot glue gun to fasten materials for students. Likewise, while a project may call for leather cord, it is feasible in most instances to substitute vinyl cord or even yarn or rope. Acrylic paint may be recommended because it adheres better to a material like felt or plastic, but other types of paint would be suitable as well. Circles can be drawn with a compass, or simply by tracing a cup, roll of tape, or other circular object. Allowing students a broad spectrum of creativity and opportunities to problem-solve within the parameters of a given project will encourage their critical thinking skills most fully.

Each project contains an italicized question somewhere in the directions. These questions are meant to be thought-provoking and promote discussion while students work on the project.

Index